Why Do You Want to Be a Worm When You Can Be a Butterfly?

by Deacon Willie Lee Walton Jr.

DORRANCE PUBLISHING CO
EST. 1920
PITTSBURGH, PENNSYLVANIA 15238

Dorrance Publishing Co
585 Alpha Drive
Pittsburgh, PA 15238
Visit our website at *www.dorrancebookstore.com*

ISBN: 978-1-6480-4589-9
eISBN: 978-1-6480-4617-9

Contents

Why Do You Want to Be a Worm When You Can Be a Butterfly?

Introduction

The purpose of this book is to support humanity in the quest for atonement with God's word to ensure proper evolutionary growth. Rather than being stagnated like a worm failing to become a butterfly, we have room for growth.

Before humanity can depart from this nomadic state to proceed toward creative innovativeness, the mind must be free.

To free a mind, it is important to obtain a logical higher order of thought and functionality to deter the stagnation of evolutionary growth.

Humanity's harmony with the environment and the faiths accordance to God's word enhances creativity.

We as Christians are sometimes faced with the problems of gathering a good understanding of this faith even after reading our Bibles. It has been said more than once that every time we read our Bible over, we gather more enlightenment towards the understanding of the word.

There is not a claim that these few words are your guide towards the clarity of God's words, but the understanding and interpretation of the Doxology coming from a humble believer's heart. We should all read our Bibles and allow the Holy Spirit to give us our motivational guidance.

These words are only for encouragement to draw you closer to believing in the faith.

God in His Infinite Wisdom Overcame the World

We should all acknowledge that God is good and very good. As we walk with the spirituality of Christian faith, in this day you shall find love, peace, grace, mercy and joy.

All these things are in place because our father has gone ahead of us and prepared this place for us. Now, in that instance when you allow the world to interrupt your atonement with the spirit of the Lord and your meditation becomes dismantled and darkness becomes a part of your day, the actual interruption becomes your god. At this point jealousy, lust, hatred, worry, enviousness, slavery, death and destruction becomes a part of your living and the rage of the outcome is totally unpredictable. So today let's all pray for the spirit of atonement with that of what thus said the Lord. He's everywhere and we are His children.

In life we must know that all material things that you own are temporary. Only the word of God will withstand the test of time. Continue to believe and show ownership and tell what you have found. His gifts are eternal. We should know that as people of faith, serving a God that stepped out on nothing and made something, a God that can supply all of our needs, a God that can make a way out of no way, a God that owns all things, a God that is Mr. Fix-It, a God that will come when we need Him, a God that has the Omnipresence, a God that arose with all of the power of Heaven and Earth in His hands, and a God that really loves His children, will always stand in the gap when there is chaos and confusion. We as a people must not worry or be in despair regarding the dilemmas that we are exposed to, know that these things are the essence of mankind's unfaithfulness and shall dissolve within itself with the passage of time. Continue to study the word and believe and know that God is able. He knows where He wants us when He wants us there! I must declare before you this day that this is a day that the Lord has made and that we must rejoice and be glad in it.

The Child's Innocence Spirit

Has your child made you smile today with his or her innocence? Try not to corrupt them with the world in you and frequently they will make you smile. One of God's greatest creations next to the world is the child. They come to us humble, peaceful, receptive, loveable, attentive, graceful, strong, and adaptive.

We can easily say that this was us, but not today because of the way that we have handled problems that we've encountered, the world has changed us. Currently, we are full of knowledge, aggressive, arrogant, egotistic, blind, impulsive, impotent, and destructive. Now, does anybody think that it's time for a change out there? How about a change for forgiveness and Love, there's lots to go around! Always search the Holy Scriptures. It is in them that you will find peace, love, mercy, grace, humbleness, and meekness all for a more atoned personality, and spirit.

Check Your Spirit to See if You…

1. Want others to fear you

2. Want to do harm to others

3. Want to enslave others

4. Want to practice black magic

5. Want to take advantage of the weak

6. Want to surrender yourselves to less than Holy things

7. Think that you are God.

If so, you may want to rethink your disposition!

Proverbs 20:11 reads: "Even a child maketh himself known by his doing, whether his work be pure, and whether it be right." Psalms 45:16: "Instead of thy fathers shall be thy children, whom thou shalt make princes in all the earth."

A mind less the corruption of the world is pure and close to the Lord. It's a part of God's Design to save the children.

Philippians 1:6: "Being confident of this very thing, that he which hath begun a good work in you will perform it until the day of Jesus Christ." It appears that the world is coming apart at the seams, so let's all attempt to be more positive in our thoughts.

We must always give thanks to God for his mercy and grace for keeping us, it's not that we deserve this, but through His forgiving grace that He allowed it. Had we received what we really deserved, none of us would be here today! As believers we must focus on God's plan for our lives rather than man's plan. Having a friend with this degree of Omnipresence as our Father in Heaven does actually make it logical to allow this theism to be our guiding light in life as the world continues to change. To be dedicated to the Divine nature of the Omnipotent power of a theocracy that desires peace, mercy, and love is exactly where our parents would desire us to be.

The dynamics of this existence simply warrants an humble mind with a pure heart. Let's focus on God's plan rather that our plan.

When we reach that point in our existence and notice prosperity in a positive nature, consider some positive perspectives in life.

Positive Perspectives

Love family regardless.

Never desire material things before God.

Pray to God daily.

Stand for something.

Train your children to honor God's will.

Help somebody every chance you get.

Learn to forgive.

Talk to God about your Pastor and his works that he might be blessed.

Love all that you have of your parents.

Treat your body as a Temple.

Mind your own business. Build strong families.

Show love to your neighbors.

Allow God to judge!

Love the Church. Study your Bible.

Never take for granted the next minute.

Lack of a positive prospective results in negativity. There is always darkness on this path.

Mankind Should Receive God as God

There is only one God, and he has the power, He is everywhere at all times and he knows all things. God is truly the only one able to judge. Mankind should turn all of his worldly concerns over to the altar of Christ and trust in him. Believe this, and the strength of your salvation for eternity will be heighten. During these enlightening stages of our missionary journeys within our faith, some of this great degree of logic is obtained, and some blessings will come, but darkness still accompanies life. It is apparent that the simple rules of a prosperous existence may not be enthusiastic enough to clear away these obstacles deterring clear thinking. God's grace is for us, prosperity in love should be our goal; yet we desire to be worldly people and do worldly things, sometimes taken, sometimes seeking. True wisdom comes from the Lord. It is our worldly ways that traps us into darkness and confusion. We should dedicate our lives to the will of Jesus Christ, He has the key to our salvation. Throughout history man has created problems for himself by being out of accordance with God's will. He frequently tries to place himself higher than God. Out of accordance with God's will, he does evil things to others, he's judgmental, and he commit sins with no intent to love others. During these points of man's existence, God is not happy or pleased with his servants as believers. The simplicity of God means that God is not complex, compound, nor is He the author of confusion. The essence of God is that it is not possible for man to know all that God knows because man's understanding is finite, whereas God's understanding is infinite. This is why we must approach God's throne of grace as a learning child.

God's Love

What is it that you think that you have that you can take with you when you leave this place and be happy and at peace, what is it that you love endlessly, that you think won't ever leave you, what is it that you care about that will be with you regardless of your situation? Your Cardinal nature will always give you the wrong answers, money, possessions, fame, friends or family. People, the true answer is God 's LOVE. Once you except it, it's there!!!

Within your growth into maturity in this faith, you must realize that love is the key to the peace of all things. We must understand that God is love, and we need to be Christlike. During your trials, in the right state of mind you shall receive protections from on high. Like the Hebrew Boys in the fiery furnace, King David against his giant, Moses and the Red Sea, and even the Apostles Peter, Paul and Silas during their death sentences, all were protected because of their love of Christ. When you find yourself expressing less than love within any communications, be aware that darkness is out there and will portray you as less than you are. What follows is chaos and confusion and these things are not of God! So be aware, love is the key. Study the word of God to show yourselves approved. Make attempts to gather atonement with this aspect of your faith. To God be the Glory.

Our God is a God of love, mercy, peace, forgiveness, meekness, giving, and grace. We must realize that these ways are the ways of a confident King that is full of blessings. Let's make straight the ways of the Lord that we might walk in Heavenly ways. Give God the praise because he is worthy to be praised. Living in accordance to his word yields blessings. We as followers should really appreciate our Father in Heaven and the fact that He rose on the third day, because of this fact, the stain and fear of death is abolished, and the gift of eternal life is forever. To God be the glory! It is important that we acknowledge the fact that at the point of conversion, if we approached the throne of grace as empty vessels waiting to be filled, a new birth shall emerge full of the Holy Spirit nurtured by the word of God. Our state of mind should be full of love, mercy, joy and peace. Unfortunately, it is evident that many of our friends partially surrendered themselves at conversion resulting in lives filled with chaos and confusion. There are signs of those that after this partial conversion, having desires of judging humanity as if God needed help. Some even feel that after this type of conversion that they possess some degree of manipulative power over humanity. Totally illogical in this theism. These problems may have come from the darkness brought to their conversion. You must be born again. As of this day, we must all understand that we serve a God that has all of the power all of the time, He is everywhere at all times and He knows all things. As for as needing help from you or me, no, He's got this!

Peace in the Garden

Why isn't the world today like the Garden of Eden was? It was design to be full of peace, joy, mercy, trust, forgiveness, love, giving spirits, graceful with understanding. Mankind has allowed the world to corrupt his spirit of atonement with this peace and it has created what you see today.

As corrupt persons, your children have probably learned corrupt things. As a parent and mentor, darkness will have an opportunity to spread when children learn from adults that are trapped. The world offers so many different paths to follow and many appear good but are simply out of the Will of God.

Let's try to build foundations that will change the world to a better place. Develop your faith in the Lord and live by it. You will notice a change. This will help with the preservation of humanity! We should all try utilizing the Holy Spirit's presence, knowledge and power as a guide. From the beginning of time logicians have concluded that in order to ensure mankind's progressive evolutionary development, he simply must surrender himself to a higher order of existence. Lack of obedience will and always has slowed God's grace and power delivered to us from on high and has altered with stagnation humanities development. We should all enjoy a more peaceful existence. Make friends with Jesus.

Destiny

As man's evolutionary journey continues
May the Lord God allow our minds to be free
That we might do God's Will
May the Lord God all ow our hearts to be humble
That we might perform selfless acts
May the Lord God allow our consciousness to be full of mercy
That we might protect the poor and the needy
May the Lord God allow his grace to be upon us
That we might be a blessing to others
May the Lord God allow His Omnipotence to be for us
That we might have a guiding light for salvation
May the Lord God al low prosperity in love to be our goal
That we might not allow worldly prosperity to destroy our souls
May the Lord God allow the Holy Spirit to be with us
That we might be an encouragement for all of mankind
May the Lord God all ow a blessing to come upon his kingdom
That we might give thanks towards truth and enlightenment

Characteristics of Trust

Trust is the confidence born of the character and the believed competence of a person or organization to express the integrity of honesty. God's will to enhance the nature of the Theism is trustworthy. Choose your friends wisely. Remember grace, love, peace, mercy, and humility all place the heart on accord with God's words. Stay close to the Church. It would not hurt your existence to make Church functions part of your lives. The Logic behind the Church helps to develop the essence of your natural state of mind which ascends directly into your evolutionary growth. In all that you do, place God first and forsake all others and you shall be enlighten toward the purpose of your very existence. We all have desires for a more prosperous existence, and we all deserve this. A few characteristic key points to enhance these desires are, the oath of innocence, the aim of moral purity and honesty, fair treatment to the poor, rejection to materialism and idolatrous worship, kind dealings with enemies, and the confessing of sins.

Knowledge of God's Goodness and Forgiving Grace

Implement these measures into your existence and in time you shall see prosperity and peace while steering away from the shadows of darkness and maturing within your faith. Remember, Jesus is the light of the world. If two bright lights shined amongst mankind, one would cause the other to cast a shadow due to a lesser brilliant illumination. Shadows are dark silhouettes of objects projected from a light source. Since Jesus is the light of the world, the purity of this light cannot be casted as a shadow. His Omnipotence illumines of the theism causes all other illuminations to cast illogical shadows of darkness. Let's continue to study the life and mission of Jesus Christ and the Theology that follows His name.

A child once asked, how do I know right from wrong? In the book of Luke Chapter 11 verses 34/35, these words express how you can determine right and wrong.

34 "The light of the body is the eye: therefore when thine eye is single, thy whole body also is full of light; but when thine eye is evil, thy body also is full of darkness."

There is darkness in greed, jealousy, lust, the lying tongue, the angered spirit, in judging others, when one places people or things higher than God.

All these things create obstacles to deter a man's clear thinking, which takes our minds away from where God wants it to be. If our minds are free, it is in our nature to do the right thing. And humble mind can do great things in the sight of the Lord.

35 "Take heed therefore that the light which is in thee be not darkness."

Walk in his way! In dealings with others, at parting, there should be joy in the hearts of all participants. Else, possibly darkness was present. Atonement to God's word yields blessings. God's grace is for us!

Theism Journals

Has anybody received notification,
That our lives are the results of creation,
Which was a part of God's glorification,
Indicating the greatness of His sanctification,
Bought and paid for in His name with justification,
All placed before us simply for our salvation,
Yet some of us have had observations,
That there are quite a few indications,
With many classifications,
That on the horizon there is devastation,
With great implications towards condemnation,
Now at some point there was an infiltration,
That resulted in this mobilization,
Which in no doubt was the verification
Of the process of elimination,
But through our Faith's maturation,
We receive strength for adaptation,
Through His power from assimilation,
We simply must resist temptation,
For the Preservation of Mankind

Take Notice to the Angered Spirit

1. It will keep you from being blessed by the Holy Spirit because of your state of mind.
2. It will not allow Jesus to handle your problems at the Altar as your Savior.
3. It will not please God by not doing His will.
4. It will take time away from your maturing within your faith while trying to solve problems with your cardinal nature.
5. It will remove the love in you and replace it with revenge, deceit and a temporary joy.
6. It will hide the Light of the world due to lack of atonement with God's grace.
7. It will not allow the Holy Spirit to monitor your next steps simply because of the darkness that exists.

This thing is as old as mankind and will project Christians improperly with darkness. Be mindful of the angered spirit's existence. There are many errors in decision making which are often the results of our choices being made while trapped in darkness. Usually the results under the conditions of these choices are a temporary joy which creates a difficulty to choose the straight and narrow ways of life over the broad ways. True joy comes from the Lord and it is everlasting. We should read the word of God to help keep us on the straight and narrow ways of life. This will help us to build a solid rock foundation. Let's try to stand for something, because it appears that we are falling for anything. Follow good leadership, it makes a strong prosperous and happy group. Leaders can only have control over themselves because we are individuals with free thinking minds, not slaves. It's a new day. Good leaders are good listeners, motivators, open and caring, discrete, good communicators, innovators and always willing to help. Bad leaders are often invisible, have poor people skills, don't often reward mentors, micro managers, manage by intimidation, and are just not appreciative.

Leadership and Guidance

Leadership is the ability to influence someone's personality. We should all try to be good leaders. Seek great leadership in your Pastors and their staff members. It is needed to develop a strong and prosperous society.

Come to Sunday School because we teach the Bible, we prepare students with better ways to face the problems of life, we teach obedience and respect for parents and those in authority, it gives students the chance to develop a relationship with Jesus Christ, it helps to build character, it presents the opportunity to share Christian experiences with peers, it offers more clarity to understanding the word, it brings together those peers that you can form a true friendship with, it gives you the chance to invite a friend to share a positive experience and it expresses to your parents that you heard something that they said.

We all must simply agree that regardless of what ever happen today it was a good day because we received it. Now at some point that only God knows, our last day will arrive, are we ready to receive it?

During the Last Days, What Will You Present to God

1. Have you matured within your faith enough to do God's will?

2. Has your choices in this life allowed your minds to be free?

3. Are the bodies that you received at birth in good order, will God receive them in good order?

4. Is humanity better off since your exposure?

5. Would you like to take with you more than you came with?

6. Would you like to start over again from day one?

7. At any point in time, did you ever fill alone?

In so many ways you can find the answers to these questions in Jesus.

Walking in the Will of God

When Jesus returns, He will want to know who has received His words and used this theology to determine guidance in their lives. There should be evidence shown from the blessings. We should all give Him praise.

One moment in Heaven a boundary sample was set up to determine what to look for to see who really had received the true words of The Lord and had instilled it in their hearts. A message of life was presented to a mass of Angels and it told what was good and very good, also what was not pleasing in the sight of The Lord. Of this mass, 100% recited Amen!!! As the Lord's heart was being blessed, a doubter appeared and said, you will never get this response from on earth because these are yours. It really looks like the people on earth are looking at something else. Now the Lord thought, have they not heard my words, will they not do my will, perhaps a test, and this doubter must not interfere. So The Lord searched His prayer log to choose a servant to bring a short message of guidance to a small group on earth and to ensure that this doubter and his friends didn't interfere, The Lord placed a powerful prayer in his servants heart that delivered the power to freeze the Devil still so that The Lord's servant could be heard. The day of the servant's message was a good day. The message was delivered with clarity and authority lacking confusion, only expressing The Lord's Will for his people. The servant was sure that the people heard the message because he noticed that all eyes were focused on him. The last words were, I hope this helped somebody mature within their faith. Now, ironically those were the last words spoken. Not a sound nor any movement for a minute, you could hear a pin drop! Blessed be to God there was a man, a descendant from one of the first men on earth, he realized that there was an issue, so he attempted to reach them as he appealed to their Cardinal nature, at this point men were attentive. The Lord was watching and thought, have they not have heard my word, are these not my servants? Who was in that room?

When your Pastor preach and you agree, please say Amen.

Free Your Mind

People, if you do wrong, and you know that it's wrong even before you do it, you probably have a new best friend who knows you better than you know yourselves.

Possibly your new best friend is the Devil itself. Free your minds; try Jesus!!! Have you ever taken the time to think of what would life be like without God's grace? You would actually be walking blind. Allow the Holy Spirit to see where you are going before you get there. This ability and power are a part of God's Omnipresence. There are plenty of traps waiting for you in darkness. Some designed just for you. Don't be a victim of your own circumstances. Accept Jesus today for a better tomorrow. Most young people look at freedom as getting out of their parents houses and doing whatever their hearts desires are. But there is a bigger picture.

During these enlightening stages of our journeys through life seeking spiritual maturity, you will encounter many opportunities to become slaves to man's ways, financial economic prosperity, vanities, greed, drugs, lust, sin and much more.

Slavery: submission to a dominating influence, lack of free will, and many other definitions all lacking expressions toward a graceful existence. Our ancestry indicates that blood, sweat and tears were exposed by our fore parents in order that we could experience freedom from slavery. It was only through Christ Jesus that they were successful. The teaching of Jesus gives us the keys to the meaning of a peaceful life filled with a joy that no man can take away, and will help us to develop our faith and spiritual maturity. These things can offer us a sense of stability in a forever-changing world because The Lord's Word's will stay the same. When people allow mankind and his world to become the driving forces over their lives, they become worldly people. We are all descendants of Abraham and are all God's children. We should set our dispositions by the eternity of the high order of the logic of our Lord and Savior, Jesus Christ. The Lord wants all mankind to have free will so that when He needs to use us as messengers, teachers and deacons all instrumental in the up building of His kingdom, mankind needs to be ready to serve with all of his heart. There are many choices in life. Be a slave to no one, let nothing take you away from where God wants you to be. Keep life simple, choose the straight gate over the broad gate.

MATTHEW 7:13, 14

13. "Enter ye in at the strait gate: for wide is the gate, and broad is the way, that leadeth to destruction, and many there be which go in thereat:"

14. "Because strait is the gate, and narrow is the way, which leadeth unto life, and few there be that find it."

In life seek your free will because you are special. We should all seek to enter at the straight gate which leadeth to life. This is the only way that Jesus will be pleased with you. God designed man in His own image; Jesus Christ was never a slave to anyone or anything.

The Gifts from the Study of God's Word

The best things in life are free simply because the study of our Lord and Savior Jesus Christ will cost you nothing. We as Christians have to realize that in order for us to mature within our faith, we must build upon a solid foundation. The Bible is sound doctrine about the life of Jesus, his love, his mercy, his grace, his peace, and his power. It is our duty as Christians to help those seeking Jesus in any way that we can. Our faith in Jesus Christ creates moral stability. It helps to have this prior to experiencing the temptations of the world. It simply is a requirement for the successful resistance from sin.

One of the biggest errors in the new converts decision making is in thinking that they can come before the Throne of Grace with a glass half full of their old nature trying to be filled with the spirituality and atonement of this Theism's Divine knowledge. The purity is not there. This only makes a weak convert.

However, an empty glass being filled with His Grace has all of its content on one accord, can build a new and worthy servant! This degree of atonement will allow the Holy Spirit to lead them to their blessings.

There is a blessing waiting for you!

The greatest degree of a servant of God's motivational thoughts are derived from situational exposure. Christians should never adjust their atonement with the true purity, Divine nature and spirituality of this faith after negative worldly exposure. This simply interferes with your blessings!!! 1 Timothy 1:1, 2: "Paul, and Apostle of Christ Jesus according to the commandment of God our Savior, and Christ Jesus our hope; unto Timothy, my true child in faith: grace, mercy, peace, from God the Father and Christ Jesus our Lord." Continue to heed to the WORD. Be ye not conformed to this world! Be blessed with this solid ROCK!!!

Part of judgment is determined when God watches our motivation. When the Bible teaches us that the poor will be with us always, this is an indicator that throughout our lives at some point we will be exposed to the poor and the needy. Selfless acts show a pure heart during our exposure to the needy which show humility, love, compassion, and obedience to God's word. God is love and He is in our hearts. Jesus is the light of the world. Have you allowed the world to change you and remove God's love from your heart.? Let's try not to be that person that kicks a man while he is down, or to be that person with an abundance and not share with the poor, or be that one who wants to keep the word to himself and not share it with our peers. When we serve God. It's about responding to a person in need. We must understand that as believers, we glorify God every time we serve anyone of God's creations.

Mathew 5:16, 43, 44, and 48, all utilize the telling of how the Lord desires us to be after conversion, and the expressions of how good God has been to Christians, 16 reads: "Let your light so shine before men, that they may see your good works, and glorify your Father which is in heaven." 43: "Ye have heard that it hath been said, Thou shalt love thy neighbor, and hate thine enemy," 44: "But I say unto you Love your enemies, bless them that curse you, do good to them that hate you, and pray for them which despitefully use you, and persecute you," and 48 reads: "Be ye therefore perfect, even as your Father which is in heaven is perfect."

You have to understand that Jesus gave the ultimate sacrifice for our salvation. You can't beat God's giving.

Doing God's Will

It is so great how God blesses us throughout the generations when we make attempts to do the right thing. You should know that if all bodies were on the same accord and doing God's will, it would seem like what you hear about Heaven. In Our faith, it indicates that if you try to do good and you are in the will of God, you will produce good. However, if you live and do evil you will produce evil and are in danger of hell's fire. Now the flavor of evil can be interesting yet it is always temporary in relations to true joy in any degree. Grace be unto thee that do God's will. Is there a blessing for you in this logical theism?

MATTHEW 7:18-20:

18 "A good tree cannot bring forth evil fruit, neither can a corrupt tree bring forth good fruit."

19 "Every tree that bringeth forth not good fruit is hewn down, and casted into the fire."

20 "Therefore by their fruits ye shall know them."

Lots of problems are occurring today in the lives of Christians that have people in their circle that they simply just do not know. Do you know who your friends are? Remember evil is out there and wants to kill your joy. Always in life preserve true joy which will lack confusion and will be a blessing from above.

There are many cultures on the planet that have percentages of citizens per geography lessor than that of the United States, yet they offer more gratitude and homage to the Divine and Pure nature of this faith, yet we are more blessed. The word tells us in Matthew 26:27, 28: 27 "And he took the cup, and gave thanks, and gave it to them, saying, Drink ye all of it;" 28: "For this is my Blood of the new testament, which is shed for many for the remission of sins." Now being a true believer, you must realize the blessing. What a friend we have in Jesus.

Since we have our instructions, and we are much more blessed than anybody else, there is simply no excuse. We the people should really work on our praise levels since we are enjoying the greatest of freedoms and the most prosperity of economic status on the planet. The world is forever changing yet Jesus stays the same!

When the Devil Attacks

Evil and darkness will approach you while trying to do God's will. This has been happening for years. Stay steadfast and immoveable within your faith. Do not surrender to your cardinal nature for revenge, lust, greed, or enviousness, at this point the Devil has you. Do not be a part of two Devil's fighting each other because they will always go to hell. Don't ever interrupt your blessings by being out of accordance with God's will, it's simply just not worth it. Turn all of your problems over to the Altar of Christ and leave them there. Stand on your faith and watch the hand of the Lord work. Do not be possessed and pretend to believe, be warned. Do not interrupt the mission of God's children. When you spend time missing out on the blessings from family, friends, and acquaintances due to something that has occurred in history, you may be considered delusional thinking that you can change history!

Stop wasting good quality time worrying about what happened yesterday. You are missing out on some important stuff. Learn today the blessings of forgiveness, and to live and love for a better tomorrow.

How Can We Judge a Man?

Can you judge a man by the actions of his cardinal nature?

Can you judge a man by his actions taken from his directions from the church?

Can you judge a man by his mistakes of the past?

Can you judge a man as a result of viewing his sinful nature?

Can you judge a man if he does not believe?

Can we judge a man for his love of money?

Can we judge a man for the neglect to his family?

Since men cannot be everywhere

at all times and does not know all things or has no power to change man's heart.

Keep peace and joy in your heart!

Pray to God for understanding!

Trust in God, He knows the heart!

God can only judge!

Playing Church

GOD is not pleased when we play Church. The Church has a job to do. Just because we attend church once or twice a week; shout Hallelujah, sing songs of praise, give support but not cheerfully, pray fast and insincere prayers, and follow all the protocols of churching; the Apostle Paul in 2 Timothy 3:5 identifies us this way: "Having a form of godliness, but denying the power thereof." Let us inventory our form of churching. Christ Jesus our Lord might identify us with the church goers in Revelation 3:15,16; addressing the Christians at Laodiceans, saying: 15 "I know thy works, that thou art neither cold nor hot: I would thou wert cold or hot."   16 "So then because thou art lukewarm, and neither cold nor hot, I will spue thee out of my mouth." The solution to playing church is found in John 4 vs. 23, 24, as Christ Jesus instructed the Christians: 23 "But the hour cometh, and now is, when the true worshippers shall worship the father in spirit and in truth: for the Father seeketh such to worship him." 24 "God is a spirit: and they that worship him must worship him in spirit and truth." We must pray to God before, during, and after our worship experience as King David did in Psalm 51:10, 13: 10 "Create in me a clean heart, O God: and renew a right spirit within me." 13 "Then will I teach transgressors thy ways; and sinners shall be converted unto thee." There is no doubt that when we as Christians play church, God sees us.

God's power is spiritually divine in nature and is design to support the good of God's plan. Man's power is cardinal in nature and is design to support the good of man's plan.

The survival of mankind must be entrusted in God's hands rather than man's because God's grace is eternal whereas man's grace is temporary. Man's knowledge is finite whereas God's knowledge is infinite.

The deceit in man's heart will cast a shadow of chaos and darkness on our existence. Jesus is the light of the world and this light will never be casted as a Shadow of darkness, only peace, harmony, and atonement. Trust in God, his grace is sufficient to supply our needs.

What Happens after Birth?

A major change in the status of humanities existence is birth. Experiencing a new environment that initiates an ability to adapt to our surroundings realizing a significant degree of power from where you came from to protect you in your new environmental conditions. You see, God didn't bring us just to leave us.

The initial building of your foundation is significant to your exposures in life. When you learn corruption, live corruption, you become corrupt people. God is Love.

There is peace when we learn about love, live with this love, we then actually reflect this love. This is expressed in a parent's protectiveness over their children's environmental exposures.

Life should be in accordance with God's plans to avoid the world's evils. Yet life offers many obstacles to interrupt God's Grace. This places us in harm's way when we utilize motivation outside of God's will. This has been a problem for many centuries. God didn't bring us this far just to leave us. Make great attempts to walk in His way, He will be your guide. The Altar of Christ is yours. Ask and ye shall receive.

Simplicity

Often, we are not quite receptive

Of our personalities being very corruptive

At times we get so aggressive

That we lose track of our objectives

Life, liberty and the pursuit of happiness was our perspective

Yet our attitude about the good things has become corrosive

As a people we have become so destructive

Without any degree of a logical motive

We should consider being less insensitive

Which might help us to be more productive

Then friends would be more responsive

In a world that can be so progressive

It's all about being more adaptive

To the way Christ wants his people to live.

You Are Never Alone

When humanities prosperity issues fully accept the concept of selfless acts, the world will change for the better, blessings will come, and this will please God. Regardless of how deep you are in the maze of darkness, if you believe, God will hear your prayers. This should tell you that you are never alone! Know of God's Omnipotent power. His will should be your driving force.

The logic behind Rev. Dr. Martin Luther King's legacy was love and nonviolence. The African-American gained much respect as his followers utilizing God's plan for his people. God is love, don't ever forget this. Soon a great leader must come forth less the ways of the world. His power will be the salvation for the people. Pray for this leadership today. We shall need it soon.

The key ingredient to our salvation is forgiveness. Grace and Faith must not be dismissed or overlooked, God loves us, even when we are dead in sin. What a mighty God we serve. Let's change our ways for better days because we have another chance.

Psalms 91:4: "He will cover you with his feathers. He will shelter you with his wings. His faithful promises are your armor and protection." Wow!!! How great is thine faith? You just need to believe!

Always take the time to love one another, never forget to count your blessings, always keep a positive perspective in order to have a great day and never forget that God will make a way out of no way!

Keep in mind that there is power in the name of Jesus!!! You must believe in him and know that he is able to move mountains and that trouble don't last always because of God's grace. Let's build on an immovable faith in His name.

Live a peaceful life, trust in God, don't worry about the world because God's got it.

The unquenchable faith of Job inspires us to trust in the Lord because His strength is great. We as Christians should fear God's power and obey God's words.

Again, don't worry about the world because God's got it.

The Presence of a Good Heart

If you can find it in your heart to commit a selfless act, a blessing will come your way. Our Father in Heaven does this every day. John 15:12: "This is my commandment, that ye love one another, as I have loved you." This is God's way. While maturing within our faith we should try to be more Christlike.

Friendship is essential for the quintessential peace of the sole.

How often in your world do you hear people saying, "I don't care" or "Ain't nothing being done that ain't been done before," or "Stop telling lies because they will catch up with you." Friends, care about everything!!! You know that God is great, and Heaven is perfect and flawless. Try your best when you come to the house of worship to have the desire to be a saint.

MATTHEW 11:23:

"And thou, Capernaum, which art exalted unto heaven, shalt be brought down to hell: for if the mighty works, which have been done in thee, had been done in Sodom, it would have remained until this day."

Care about the world that you are building because it's all about you and God's forgiving grace, another chance! God will not allow you to start trouble in Heaven!

The greatest part of our faith is expressed during the times when we believe in and are obedient to our Father which is in heaven. You must know that this is where we receive our strengths. Just think that if you didn't know of His forgiving grace, your life would be filled with conflicts. If you didn't know that He rose, you couldn't see the light of day. If you didn't know of His Omni Spirit, Agape Love, Omnipotence, Omnipresent, all-seeing, all-knowing Grace, you wouldn't have the nerves to step out on faith. You should also understand that if you didn't know of the powerful miracles that He performed, you wouldn't know that anything is possible. God is great and God is Good!

Let's believe and achieve.

Maturing within the Faith

You know that once you've gotten your mind set
This means that you've passed the test
That you wanted to be free from stress.
That you walked off and left the rest
Because you simply wanted to be blessed
By none other than the Best!

The Problem with Putting Faith on a Shelf at Your Convenience

Do you guys have any friends that have a degree of Faith that is sometimes placed on a shelf at their convenience only to reach back for it on Sunday mornings? Warning, this attitude is contagious, you are what you allow your associates to make of you! Since our Father in Heaven will never change, you in your Faith should never allow the world to change you. Stand on the solid rock of Jesus 24/7. Express to your friends the love that you have for your Faith, at this point, you and their existing deceitful Logic will have parting ways along with the chaos and confusion. Know that God is love, and you should recognize it when you see it. Be blessed with His grace!!

A child should never separate himself from the love of his parents because at that point he can receive no help. The same thing occurs within a Christian's life when his faith is not constant. At this point he is not covered by the blood of Jesus. Stay steadfast and immovable within your faith. God loves you.

Your state of mind should never outweigh your faith. If you lose your possessions and your steady income ceases to exist and the love of your life is not putting up with it, stand on your faith. Pray and leave the problems at the Altar of Christ and know God's got it. God's grace is all that you need.

There is an anointing in the child that recognizes the day of atonement is vastly approaching with significant signs as evidence of the change. You see, God can allow mankind to only go so far away from his plan of existence, then the trumpets will sound, and atonement will come. Leviticus 23 in its entirety offers some clarity and understanding of what is potentially about to converge upon humanity. Mankind needs to stop trying to be God and simply follow

His plan of salvation for humanity. There he shall find peace, joy, love, mercy, forgiveness, understanding, and friends!

Our world does not signify this graceful nature because of the things that we are doing to ourselves and others. It's time for a change for better days. It is through the love of God that the wicked sinners will not overcome a child that believes. The transgressions of the sinner show no fear of God. The sinner's hateful ways offer astonishing pride and are iniquitous with deceit. But God!!! Our Savior's Omnipotence is our salvation. Just believe and step out on faith and watch the hand of the Lord move mountains. God is good!

God's Grace

You know that you have been blessed when you are not concern if a deceitful heart is in your presence, or you feel that a lie is being told to you or on you, or that person that you had considered a friend had a hidden agenda with no love for you. When you convert to a degree of Faith and leave worldly issues to the worldly people, you shouldn't be concern with worldly behavior. Know that it's God's Will to judge our iniquities. Your job is to share the love of God in you. Continue to watch because God's got control of all things.

The true Ares of Being. Greater is He that is in me than he that is in the world. His forgiving grace surpasses all things. It truly gives life to this Agape love. For mankind is weak and He is mighty. His power is infinite. Blessings will come when we fear God! One soul, one man, one God! There is nothing like the joy in the hearts of those that believe in our Father which is in Heaven when exposed to the troubles of the world and the people in it.

Want to be blessed, try Jesus! Then, the world won't change you.

In man's hands, this world is turning into a bucket of chaos and confusion. You know two Devils will stand and fight all day. If humanity only realized that sometimes we find ourselves off the straight and narrow paths because we are weak! Only the Lord can fix this if it were placed in His hands! His mercy and grace reveal the temporary joys in the hearts of those that know and love Him. Some folks should just try Jesus!!!

Does any of you have friends with deceitful hearts, that are not trustworthy, that are not helpful in times of crisis, that are not very loving people, that you don't really want them around your family, that you wouldn't allow them to stay at your home, that you cannot tell everything, that you cannot trust with your life or that you've had the thought of why do I even deal with this person? The thing to do when you have these types of friends is to try Jesus as a friend and tell your other friends about Him.

Watch miracles occur within your lives as lots of your problem simply just go away!

It was on that day that the people of little faith did not believe that the Lord reached out into nothing and created something, the people that exhausted themselves in sin and darkness thinking that they had something, fell asleep in their faith, awakening finding that there was nothing! Believe and receive!

You should know that when you are blessed with kids, their divine nature makes them quite intelligent the first days of their lives. Most of the problems that people have with their kids are from the things that people teach them. Good things in good things out, bad things in bad things out. Try to add to the strong survival traits that a child is graced with through the divine nature of Jesus Christ. This will help the child's appreciation for life more abundant and will be pleasing in the sight of the Lord.

Only by the grace of God, some of us have a freed state of mind, not anchored in darkness, not enslaved or challenged. Isn't it ironic that people with these blessings still sin? One could consider these actions as lack of faith! When you know that God has the power and with His Omnipresence, you must understand how fast things can change. Be thankful for your blessings.

Grace be unto thee that love ye the Lord, His mercy is everlasting, His love is unending, His grace is forever, His presence is always on time. Keep on believing that you can keep on receiving His blessings from on high. Trust in Him, He is able! Had it not been for His forgiving grace, things just would not be the same. Let's take a little time out to say thank you Jesus because events could have gone another way. That agape love, that eternal mercy because the flush is weak, and that everlasting grace is true salvation. Love, mercy and grace, might we offer a lesson in spiritual dynamics? The word says that it is better to give than to receive, many give but with and attitude. The true telltale story is that everything belongs to the Lord! What you have God has only allowed you to use possibly because of something that you did right spiritually. You can go ahead and cancel that U-Haul contract because you leave as you came. Everything goes back to the owner.

Why Do You Want to Be a Worm When You Can Be a Butterfly?

Any society that does not value the true Ares of Being degrees of logic, moral, ethical or spiritual charismatics, is destined to destroy itself because of the lack of love and commitment to one another. Jesus saves! He offers us the plan of salvation. The true essence of life. We should give Him the time and the praise!

By the grace of God, we are still here. The question is, are we grateful? Most parents will do almost anything for their children, yet children sometimes break house rules creating disenchantment causing them to suffer punishment. News flash, the same thing happens to our Father in Heaven. Understand that for God's will to work in our lives, we must follow His rules. He wants to bless us with gifts, but we must stay on accord with Him and know that He loves us and is able to supply our needs. Let's all try not to break God's rules that we shall not be punished. Remember He is Omnipresent and Omnipotent and owns all things! The understanding of these rules comes from the studying of the Holy Bible and sharing by attending study groups.

Obedience yields stability. "We hold these truths to be self-evidence that all men are created equal"; these words are a part of the preamble to the Constitution, which was designed by a faithful group that created a community of love and brotherhood. Yet the original design has been tainted by the darkness of mankind's illogical thoughts as we walk in this sinful nature. We must be obedient to the words in the Holy Bible that tells us to pray without ceasing, else we will destroy ourselves; friendship is essential for the preservation of mankind! Be blessed today, know of your heritage.

As much as we love the way things are in our lives, it's not you, it's just Jesus. Simply, if we all got what we deserved, things would not be so great. The first chance you get acknowledge the forgiving grace of Jesus Christ and thank Him for being a friend. After gathering atonement with the spirit of the faith and understanding the fact that God's Will shall be done, it will never be your will again to be motivated by or to have a desire to do worldly things. At the point in time that you acknowledge degrees of darkness as your spiritual guide, you must come to the realization that you have actually been conquered by some outside forces that has taken you away from where God needs you to be. There you shall find chaos and confusion. Once converted, stay prayed up, study God's word constantly, share with others that are studying that you might evaluate others' atonement. Always notice your perspective towards the Theological concepts. There should always be peace in the valley! You must know that God see all things, know that God is great, and God is good! Try to keep all aspects of the faith in practice and in mind at all times. Step out on faith! He will see you through your trying times. If at that point when you were converted, if your glass was empty, during trouble times, He saw you through it. Now on the other hand, during trouble times if your glass was half empty, then the world in the glass took you to it. You must depend on the Holy Spirit for peace and guidance. Two devils will fight all day without the help of Jesus!

God's love is great enough to sustain us, His power is great enough to maintain us. What a great God we serve!

There is great joy in knowing that the Lord has prepared a place for us where we can enjoy a peaceful existence, love on one another, not judge each other, support the sick and the needy, and spend time praising God all day. Need directions? Just do His will!

Have you ever been lost and after requesting directions and later finding out that they did not lead you to where you wanted to go? There are people out there that will actually give you bad directions sometimes by mistake, other times for entertainment or financial gain. Some folks are just evil.

Now there is a God that has infinite wisdom and Omnipresence that lots of believers serve. This Holy Spirit will walk into your future and show you a path. I have heard lots of stories from believers that confess to requesting directions and are placed on a path to where they were needing to be. Believers don't ever forget to call on the name of Jesus if you find yourself lost or just can't find your way. He will supply all of your needs. He has all of the power in Heaven and earth is in His hands. Be blessed today, just believe His words in the Holy Bible.

Have you ever been at your church home and became disenchanted with the personalities that showed signs of deceit, disrespect, dishonesty, disloyalty, gossiping, lying, judging and blasphemy towards the Holy Ghost, and this made you so upset that you had considered leaving the church and you wondered why!

Well, if this was you, I really hate to burst your bubble, but you really need to understand a few things:

(1). It was all your fault.

(2). It was not your business unless you are the Pastor and his staff.

(3).	You are judging folks and God is the only one able to judge.

(4).	Your job while you are at Church is to study, worship, and praise God.

(5).	In all that you think you know and understand, know this, God in His infinite wisdom and Omnipresent state, has the situation under control and always believe that He does not need any help from you!

If you are not careful, you can become the congregates that you are complaining about. Nothing but love. Study your Bible to gather and understanding of your purpose in the House of Worship.

Isn't it nice when friends or family does something special for you just because they love you? Naturally you think about them frequently and give them praise for their good nature.

Why is it that our Father which is in Heaven with all of His giving, His forgiving grace, the many blessings from His agape love, His omnipotent Holy Spirit with its ingratiating guidance, is not given worship and praise every minute for His goodness?

Common sense makes you wonder sometimes if you are truly walking the straight and narrow path where you should give recognition to your keeper. Could it be that you are just driven by some unknown entity? Be aware, Satan is out there.

Every chance you get, give God the praise simply because He is worthy! You must know that things don't have to be as well as they are for you.

When man gives you praise for worldly events, this does not mean that God's Will has been done. Every word in the Holy Bible is true and did happen. The words that are in the King James Version Bible written in red letters truly are God's Words! The grace of praise from worldly event that violates the covenant with God can be Satanic in nature according to this Theism. Praise that is received according to God's Will can be graceful on earth as well as in Heaven. Be careful about receiving praise!!!

Have you ever wondered why wealth doesn't come into your life? Actually, wealth is not for everybody because most folks can't handle it. If your heart is not right, you could block your own blessings. God knows your heart and there is nothing that you can hide from Him. Ever had the thought that if you had millions, that you would go and get the one that you missed out on when God had already given you what you needed. What about the one when you thought that if you had millions that you would get as far away from some people as possible. Failing to realize that God may have place them there and that they are the ones that are helping you hold it together. And what about the thought that if you had it you would ship your kids off to boarding school or summer camp just to get rid of them failing to acknowledge that God has granted you parenthood as a gift of perseverance? Now we don't need to talk about buying drugs, alcohol, or sex because we are just not those types of people.

To evaluate the thoughts of the things that we desire without any knowledge of the impact that such things will have upon our lives, God stands in the gap. God's grace will supply our every need. In His infinite wisdom He understands our wants and desires and has looked and seen the impact that these things will have upon our lives. God is great and God is good enough to know our needs and He and His omnipotence's will supply our needs. Worry and fears should not be a part of our living. All you have to do is believe. Always know that God is an on-time God! He will always get you what you want when you need it. Try not to interrupt your blessings with some egotistical desires to be more worldly than you need to be. As believers our inheritance to the throne of a God that owns everything where wealth is not an issue should create a settle spirit. Always enjoy what you have because somebody has always got it worse. Know that God loves you and has a plan for you.

Mankind since forever and a day has been wanting to conquer the divine nature of the faith out of enviousness and with controversy. Most of the time when we meet grown-ups that desire something that we have, they come with a hidden agenda! This is one of the reasons why when the woman asked that her son be granted a high position in the kingdom, she was denied. Jesus expressed to her that for this blessing to come, they were to approach the throne as a child and humble themselves as an empty vessel and prepared to be filled. Each day we must consider the fact that we might not make it with the world's evils in and around us. Now if you think that you don't have anything to be thankful for, consider the fact that somebody didn't wake up this morning. We are blessed in so many ways. Praise God every chance you get.

Why Do You Want to Be a Worm When You Can Be a Butterfly?

Our Father in Heaven is a healer. A good percentage of the problems of humanity are subconscious thoughts. I have found in my studies and meditation periods, that my self-conscious mind has been enhanced a great deal because so many negative thoughts have been eliminated from my being. Negativity yields darkness resulting in subconscious thoughts. Functionalities suffer because at this point, we are less than 100% of the 20/20 vision needed to view God's Heavenly designed for humanity! All a part of God's plan. Trust and believe that He wants to bless us.

God's Pride

When Jesus speaks of the children, there appears to be a since of pride in the air. A child's innocence and uncorrupted spirit is true and divine in nature and can gather atonement with the Holy Spirit. Jesus ask that we come to Him as a little child that we might inherit the Kingdom of heaven. Mankind should grow in grace not in the world. This would be pleasing in the sight of the Lord.

You know that the world is full of things to do that sparks your interest, and so is Heaven. But many things that you do on earth cannot be done in Heaven. For the eternal environment, all that is good and very good that follows God's plan of salvation for his people is acceptable and should be your living motivation. Let's try to get a good practice in today! Practice makes perfect.

Those that have been exposed to this marvelous light where the illumination has brought great exuberance with degrees of joy to their hearts, they should stay in the light. Yet the temporary joys of darkness that has the tendency to draw us away from the true atonement and grace, places us on the path of death and destruction. We really must learn to keep our eyes on the prize. Signs of a true and forgiving God. Another chance!!! If ever you encounter a day when you couldn't experience God's love, the safest thing for you to do would be to go back to sleep. I must say that this might be like that place that I heard of called Hell!!! Become a child of God. Know that God is love. God loves His children. Trust in God's love so that you want get lead into the darkness of Hell.

The World and God's Love

Indulging in the joys of love takes you out of darkness and places you into the marvelous light. Thirty-five of the Books in our Holy Bible mentioned expressions of love and many more than once. You know this love thing might have some significant to a peaceful existence. For what it is worth, money was mentioned only in ten chapters in the Bible. Wonder if this has any significance to our existence? Do you spend a lot of time wondering who's trying to get you when you got lots of money? You must know that God is love and in His infinite wisdom He holds the key to a joyful existence. Give a little love today because there is a chance that you will receive some back.

If you think on this Theism and its magnificence and the fullness of its power, you can't help but to put a smile on your face and a song in your heart. We are even blessed with gifts if we do His will. The relaxation of waterfalls, the joy of birds singing, the unexpected responses from the innocence of a young child. God is good!

Every life has encountered a point when they realized that some situations that they have been involved in, that they were unsatisfied with their actions. This happens when people live in a complex society and have not consumed any degree of logical thought to believe in. Even after acknowledging this theological degree of thought and not applying discipline warrants man's life lacking thereof. You see, in life if you don't stand for something you will fall for anything. So as of today, we should stop the Flip Wilson "Geraldine" act which implies that the devil made you do it. No, it's just you! When we don't utilize God's Love to overcome the world, we can easily find ourselves victims of our own circumstances. You see, the Holy Spirit is able to examine the results of your actions before they occur within your lives. All you have to do is believe.

Let's take a stand today, dedicate your lives as true believers and watch the hand of the Lord change your situations. All Church doors are open, and anything is possibly.

Reality Is in Jesus

Have you ever been kidnapped or abducted by a situation and realized it later? This happens more frequent than people acknowledge.

A fella once told me that he had met a lady at a club and they became friends, with thought of intimacy at her home as she return from the bathroom with a different anatomy. Was he kidnapped?

A couple was married for several years and after a slight dispute, it was revealed that there was another love that kept the spouse unhappy at home. Was someone kidnapped?

Have you ever experienced as a Christian after studying that your teacher was not teaching the true words that you had studied and you were confused, and that there was some hidden agenda, spiritual or financial, yet you were left confused? Is this a form of kidnapping?

Seems like the lust, deceit, and false teachings are the culprits in these situations with negative influences almost enough to discourage interest in life itself.

As a person of faith, I truly believe that the Holy Spirit can guide Christians through these things. Continue to study this Divine word and God will see you through. He can move mountains. Be blessed.

What a Mighty God We Serve

Thankful for having a Friend like Jesus, because He has such forgiving grace, that He is able to build us up when we are torn down, that He is able to sustain us in a world with such opposition, that He offers a solid foundation, that He can create a way out of no way, that He knows what we need when we need it, that He is able to move mountains, that His mercy will endure our pain, that His humbleness will provide us peace, that His grace is everlasting, that there is healing in His name, that He is the light of the world, that He is our salvation, that He is able to stand in the gap when we lack the strength to prevail, that there is no darkness around His throne, that there is no trickery about His business, that there is no confusion in His presence, that His love causes no chaos in life, that He allows us to leave all of our problems at the altar, that He will fight our battles, that He has this agape spirit of love which is unconditional, that He died for our sins that we might be free, that He rose with all of the power of Heaven and Earth in His hands, that He loves His children, that He provides strength to families, that He will never leave us, that He has the last word, that in order to receive Him we only have to accept and believe in Him.

When the world offers trying times for the faithful, it is always a good idea morally to offer converts comfort in knowing that God is in charge. Strength in acknowledging God's plans can move mountains. Those that believe will receive the eternal light of thoughts beyond their circumstances. Always understand and know that God moves through a precise and divine plan, that He will never leave nor forsake you and that He can make a way out of no way. Jesus is the light of the world and He's ever shining in the soles of those that receive and believe His words!

If understanding is vague, lean not on yourselves, join a Bible study group where the divinity of His word is the main subject elaborated upon which can help you to find a friend in Jesus!

Introduction To The City Myob

The city of MYOB is a city of a most peaceful existence. The city's ground area covered about seven square miles with a population of 14,400 citizens. The communities are well off peacefully with little crime. The city has one small police station with one squad car that is across the street from the only nightclub. The ideology for this geographical design was that when trouble started, the officers would not have far to travel. Nobody has ever been arrested in MYOB. It's well known that after so many incidents and warnings you could be evicted from the city.

The communities are mostly faith based from the seven local spiritual churches where you can feel God's grace, where all members trust in God's Omnipresence, and all citizens vow to live in accordance with God's will. This principle was drilled into the community citizen from its Bible-studying, Church-attending family members. In short, it was taught that God has a plan and He knows how to do his job without any assistance, and that it is the citizens responsibility to live life according to His plan.

To get to MYOB, take a left off of Faithful Circle to Temptation Boulevard, take a right on Love Lane to Straight and Narrow Drive till you see the road sign at a fork in the road that says TT pointing to the left (TT is the city of Trouble Times), it is the same size city as MYOB and four years ago the population count of citizens was close, TT has about 10,000 citizens. TT has seven police stations all strategically located, and one Church where most of the people come on Sunday to find out about who died last week! There are three police stations located inside the Church and one on each corner outside of the Church. You have to understand that every Sunday like clockwork there was going to be a fight, see this Church is where the devil will get all over you to where by the time you leave, you will have forgotten the purpose of the Church and why you came. These folks know that they are needing to change.

Common sense will tell you to stay out of TT, but the Devil and inquisitiveness will take you there before you know it. By the way, MYOB to the right stands for Mind Your Own Business! Remember, at the fork in the road, if you stay to the right MYOB will soon be in your sight.

Humanity vs. the Free-spirited Mind

After birth, the degree of intelligence that is a part of your anatomy is jeopardized by different degrees of exposure and experiences that life presents as you take this walk. The philosophical thoughts, concepts of love, even logical motivation that is practiced by your designers is simply abandoned due to lack of use as you age within most environments about this new world. Too many dark spirits.

The true doxological nature of this theological concept yields eternal salvation.

Now we can change the world, but it will take at least a couple of centuries, and it will take everybody's help. The Holy Word teaches us to not let the world change us utilizing unshakable faith. It is critically imperative that we teach children this as early as communications is possible. With the worldly clouds that have interrupted our thoughts, we have the tendency of failing to realize the intellect that very young children possess. That child comes from God, thinks like God, possesses some of God's power, and is the pride and joy of our Father in Heaven.

We should make great attempts to do our parts in creating a better world for our kids to grow in which would be pleasing in the site of the Lord. Otherwise death is imminent.

Jesus Is the Light of the World

In the day of our Lord, there are some that don't believe. Perhaps these are the ones that have not come to the realization of a day coming when vanity will be lifted up as their god's. Having no understanding that there will be no Savior to lead them through trials, tribulations chaos and confusion because they did not believe. Those that have not absorbed the spirituality of the truth have allowed their nomadic ancestry to overcome the redemption of their salvation. Simply stating, allowing deceit to be their guide not truth, hatred being their joy not love, lust being their desire not procreation and having darkness in their hearts not this marvelous Light. These shall have their day of reckoning! To God be the Glory!!!

Have you ever noticed any people that have the dark spirit of deceit, that are untrustworthy, that possesses a lying tongue, usually cannot learn because they know everything, and are filled with a negative spirit in conversation about all things, these people are trapped in darkness, offer them prayer.

Lots of people think that breaking rocks in prison is the hardest job on the planet, try convincing this type of person that their disposition is affecting their health because they are a part of the environment. The spirit of faith in Jesus Christ implies that God is and Omnipresent God. This means that He is everywhere and he knows all things. He has a plan of action for all living things. When these confused entities create worlds away from God's plan, they are no longer covered by His power, strength, wisdom and knowledge. We should all follow God's plan simply for good health. God has been good to us! With all of the freedoms and liberties that we have, we should take a minute to say thank you, Jesus, just for keeping us. We all know that things could have been a different way, but God and his forgiving grace and infinite wisdom saw fit to keep us. God knows who He wants us to be and He talks about it in His words. This divine doxology is a theology that delivers benefits when we take from the excellence of its design and apply it into our practical living. Truly it is illogical to study the word of God and not use it. There is power in the name of Jesus! We should all try harder to be what God wants us to be.

As we live and breathe, we must keep love in our hearts. This helps us to truly step out on faith. Know that God is love and we must keep Him as our guide to maintain that perfect piece. During the times that we step towards anger, vengeance, deceit or harm, we are truly in danger of hell's fire. At this point in our existence we are not pleasing in the sight of our Lord and Savior Jesus Christ. God has all of the power in His hands and he is everywhere at all times. History has recorded that his chosen people, the Israelites, were chastised because they turned away from God's love many times. Their salvation was only because of His loving and forgiving Grace. We should never tempt God! Each step that we take, we should consider all things and move towards love. With this love, God's protection can order our steps in His name. Be blessed!

Steadfast and Immoveable Faith

Don't ever let anything or anybody separate you from your accordance with God's will. At such a state, one could be in danger of hell's fire! When dark shadows over comes one of God's children and encourages them to use black magic to control another man's soul and disturb the balance of atonement that is with our Father God in Heaven, this will anger God. This Theism's Doxology indicates that we must be free spirited in order to think clearly. The pure illumination of this Faith's brilliance can never cast a shadow. Jesus is the light of the world; therefore, there is no darkness resulting from this atonement. God is love, therefore when man finds himself in this state of mind, it is truly apparent that the love of God is not there. Check yourselves, you shouldn't try His patience, you might get burned. The closer we get to Our Father in Heaven the more we see the beauty of things in this life that He has prepared for us. Isn't it amazing how when people turn away from Our Father to serve other gods, the joyful nature of life turns away from them! Atonement with His plans are easy, just follow Jesus and be blessed. If you think that God does not love you think twice! Know that everything written in the Holy Bible is true! All that we do and yet we don't get what we deserve. Isaiah 1:18-20: 18 "Come now and let us reason together saith the Lord: though your sin be as scarlet: they shall be as white as snow; though they be red like crimson, they shall be as wool." 19 "If ye be willing and obedient, ye shall eat the good of the land:" 20 "But if ye refuse and rebel, ye shall be devoured with the sword: for the mouth of the Lord hath spoken it."

The voice of the Lord shall speak unto you in your transgressions with a warning because of His love for you, understand that this is all because of His forgiving Grace that we are as well off as we are today. Continue to study the word of God, when you know better, try to do better!

Trust in the Word

One day after a storm I was driving on the highway and I came to a dip in the road that took the interstate under water for about 300 yards. Well, I knew that my car was capable of lots of things according to the instructions manual but I don't recall reading about a button to press to make the car float, so I turned around and headed on a new route to go around the water.

Now why is it that when people during their travels encounter obstacles, confusion, trials and tribulations, that they often make failing attempts to meet a resolve simply because they don't know the Lord! Our Father in Heaven has provided us with an instructions book that will safely bring us out of any bad situation with blessings for everyone that is involved. Make great attempts to read your Bible daily, this will help to limit the degree of chaos and confusion that will come your way after trying to solve problems your way rather than the Lord's way. Understand that the world's greatest instructions book is the Holy Bible. Peace be unto thee that knows the Lord's way!

The Lord's ways promote a define logical state of mind. Degrees of intellect are equal to the level of atonement with defined logical thought. Having profound self esteem, having desires of procreation, having an understanding of a significance creator, having the realization that all things have a beginning and an end, understanding that you don't know everything which signifies that you can learn something, only God knows all things! Having a good understanding of societies extroverted and introverted personalities, having significant utilization of deductive logical reasoning, knowing that levels of exposure constitutes perspective, desiring the seeding of humanities uplift through creative innovative motivation, having a true understanding of the "Ares of Being" the "Is Factors" of life, gathering a total resolve towards mankind physiological origin suppositions, and having the total control of the preoccupation from degrees of ignorance! True logical thought will enlighten your very existence. One could consider the possibility that this is Heaven's Gates or at least on the right road toward pursuance.

Is it true that the world spoils people? Before children are exposed to society, they do possess an enchantingly adorable attraction. Can you count with your fingers the number of adults that have no social obstacles that interrupt pure thinking? We are talking the strength of Priest. How amazing would it be to recognize chaos, confusion and darkness as it approaches humanity? What a mighty God we serve. The word says He rose with all of the power of Heaven and earth in his hands, He is everywhere at all times, and He knows all things. If you trust and believe, your actual world can change. Pray and ask that you become unshackle from the worldly ways that you might serve Him better. There is lots of love, peace, and prosperity on this path. Be Blessed this day!

All that You Take In Defines You

They say that you are what you eat, does this mean that when you inhale things this constitutes who you are. Does this theory support the statements that the world corrupts children? Are there some things that we are not supposed to partake of due to molecular structure or atomic protein sequencing?

The Bible tells us in Deuteronomy 14:3-21 that "You shall not eat any detestable thing. These are the animals which you may eat: the ox, the sheep, the goat, the mountain goat, the antelope, and the mountain sheep. And you may eat every animal with cloven hooves, having the hoof split into two parts, and that chews the cud, among the animals. Nevertheless, of those that chew the cud or have cloven hooves, you shall not eat, such as these: the camel, the hare, and the rock hyrax; for they chew the cud but do not have cloven hooves; they are unclean for you. Also, the swine is unclean for you, because it has cloven hooves, yet does not chew the cud; you may not eat their flesh or touch their dead carcasses.

"These you may eat of all that are in the water: you may eat all that have fins and scales, and whatever does not have fins and scales you shale not eat, it is unclean for you.

"All clean birds you may eat. But these you shall not eat: the eagle, the vulture, the buzzard, the red kite, the falcon, the kit e after their kinds; every raven after its kind, the ostrich, the short-eared owl, the sea gull, and the hawk after their kinds, the little owl, the speech owl, the white owl, the jack drawdown, the carrion vulture, the fisher owl, the stork, the heron after its kind, and the hoopoe and the bat. Also, every creeping thing that flies is unclean for you; they shall not be eaten. You may eat al l clean birds.

"You shall not eat anything that die of itself, you may give it to the aliens who is within your gates, that he may eat it, or you may sell it to a foreigner; for you are a holy people to the Lord your God. You shall not boil a young goat in its mother's milk."

Some people hear things, others see things, or feel things, or experience biological illnesses, mostly because of protein sequencing. The safest thing to do is to stay in the spirit and allow the Holy Spirit to direct your path. Be blessed today in the strength of the Lord!

It is because of mankind's state of mind, engulfed in an illogical state, that he sins. The word of God teaches us to meditate and keep our minds stayed on Jesus. When we are exposed to worldly ways, our mind often wanders into the state of why things happen. Lack of faith causes us to worry and often motivate our actions. We must know that our Father in Heaven, in His Omnipresence, and infinite wisdom has the situation under control. It is simply not our jobs to judge in this finite state. In life we must know our place, meditate on Jesus and enjoy this place that He has prepared for us. As often as you can, study and pray that God's Will be done.

Acknowledgment to Parenting

Parents prepare a home for you where you can feel safe.
Parents are there to listen when nobody else will.
Parents will love you regardless of your ill mannerisms.
Parents will teach you success from life's experiences.
Parents will lead you towards peace and enlightenment.
Parents will never leave you even after transitioning.
Parents reward you for listening to sound logic.
Parents know more about you than you do yourself.
Parents are always parents.
Parents can sometimes love you more than you love yourself.
Parents never stop thinking about you.
Parents are the evidence of some of God's greatest works.
Parents enjoy seeing themselves in you and what you do.
Parents are just like Jesus when it comes to their children.
Thank you, Jesus, for being such a great parent!
Please help us to become better children.

God's Grace Is Sufficient Enough to Supply All of Our Needs

Oh come, all Ye faithful, that we might all try to keep joy in our hearts and peace on our minds because we are wanting Joy to the World! Know that Jesus is the King of peace and we should all give The Faith a chance to order our steps in His word. There will be Blessed Assurance if we keep families first which is His way. Do these things and you will have a Silent Night!

We the people have a variety of consciousnesses. Know that in different levels of consciousness there are different level of power. Now if at that point of converting to Christianity you departed from the world's ways and surrendered unto the Holy Spirit, the power from our Father in Heaven is potentially at hand for you. However, individuals that desire to carry worldly things to Heavenly places, when you just can't let go, this will make you weak. You have to understand that your consciousness is actually serving two masters, one is weak, and one is strong. When Jesus rose, He rose with the power of Heaven and Earth in His hands! Power over worry, fear, grief, pain, deceit, enviousness, lust, anger, malice, revenge, death and much more. He can even look beyond your steps and lead you as a guide to safety. Personally, I would say let go and let God. He has the key to love, mercy, joy, contentment, grace, peace and much more.

We have those amongst us that have brought their worldly ways with them through conversion into this faith. Our first job is to pray for them, then we must teach them of the degree of darkness in the error of their ways. When one approaches the throne of grace, the purity of its divine nature will reject the darkness of worldly ways.

The power that is at hand will be limited because of degrees of atonement to the faith. Grace be unto thee that has surrendered himself to this true and divine nature of this faith, for the power is at hand. Those that carry worldly darkness after conversion, expect chaos, confusion, darkness and death. This occurs because of the illogical impurities of nature which will simply make you weak. To experience the love, peace, and grace from our Father which is in Heaven, we must learn to let go and let God!

To God Be the Glory

When you recognize friends, tell them about Jesus. Allow me to introduce you to my BFF. "Best Friends Forever," God's grace. How great is it to have a God that is willing to stand in the gap for us in trouble times? His being there really make life much simpler. His ways are ways of peace, love and forgiveness. Just think that if everyone knew and lived by His ways, life would be like one big long holiday full of joy, mercy and His grace. God's grace is enough to supply our needs. Consider the conversion from mankind's judgment to accepting God's forgiving grace, this would be the results of a better world.

After studying some theological concepts, we must envision the thought that we may be victims of our own choices. Humanity sealed with the degree of logic towards this Theism will receive victory over the opposition. Grace be unto thee that believes. These are times for celebrating His grace.

Can we look back at our lives and say that we have been as loving, giving, thankful, and forgiving as we should have been? The answer is probably not. Our Creator and Father which is in Heaven is full of these graces and did design man in His image. We have become a society caught up in possessions and material gain, which defines us. This degree of selfishness that is upon us slows down our productivity level and is an illogically learned trait from the world. The world tells us that we own things when actually everything belongs to the Lord. Job 1:21: "Naked came I out of my mother's womb, and naked shall I return tithed." This was Job's contentment after losing everything. Let's not allow our possessions define us because things deteriorate with time, only the Lord's words will stand the test of time. His ways will create a unified giving spirit in us.

One of the most difficult tasks in the life of a Disciple to Christ is to get the none believers, after surrendering themselves while standing at the door of conversion, to believe in a savior that has the ability to supply all of their needs. If one can understand that humanities dilemmas are the result of mankind's choices. Now in that same sense of logical deductive reasoning, we can conclude that successful peaceful living will be the results of the belief and guidance from a sound theological doxology. Make a choice today, the word says that you cannot serve two masters. In this lifetime you shall see the grace of His marvelous Light that is surrounded by peace and love or you will see the darkness and despair of the world that will steal your joy. Step out on faith and be blessed today, try Jesus.

The Darkness of the World

We must remember that we live in a world that is full of the darkness from mankind's sinful nature from the Garden. As we correspond with constituents as saved souls, keep in mind that God's covenant has been placed on the hearts of mankind and should be used as a filter to help us to walk in His way. Too often the mind tells the tongue to speak evil things lacking the utilization of the filtering from the heart. At this point we as Christians are labeled as evil people. We must not cut ourselves short of the love that we have surrendered unto, always utilize the filtering system in sequence, mind, heart, tongue. This helps communications to come out portraying you with the love of righteousness. We must stop speaking evil into existence, it counts against us.

There is significant evidence that your level of faith can determine the level of stress in your life. Early on in life your level of stress was low because your parents handled all progressive dilemmas. As a believer, you must know that God has all of the power in His hands, that He is everywhere at all times, that He knows all things and He loves His children. As children of the King, we don't worry about worldly issues because we already know that God has control of the situation. Worrying creates a stressful situation and this is why we, as children of the King, look so good. Take a minute to tell Jesus thank you for less stress.

When you spend time missing out on the blessings from family, friends, and acquaintances due to something that has occurred in history, you may be considered delusional thinking that you can change history! Stop wasting good quality time stressing out about what happened yesterday. You are missing out on some important stuff.

Learn today the blessings of forgiveness, and to live and love for a better tomorrow.

God's Infinite Wisdom

There is power in the name of Jesus. Humanity must understand that the more atoned your motivation is to God's will, the more power you will receive. There come times when people get God's power confused with man's power. God's power requires a lot of prayer to be a recipient and is pleasing in the sight of the Lord because of its spirituality. Man's power usually relates to some degree of wealth, bartering, or money changing with an advantage for some and others at a disadvantage. Man's power was one of the reasons that Jesus removed the money changers from the House of Prayer simply because everybody wasn't being helped. Matthew 21:13: "It is written, my house shall be called the house of prayer; but ye have made it a den of thieves." The true clarity of understanding power comes when man acknowledges that one type always yields peace while the other does not. Jesus is the author of peace.

Since the beginning of time, mankind has lost years of progressive development due to the lack of knowledge about his purpose in life. This knowledge in essence is the key to efficient living. Most people would be surprised to see the number of deterrents there are to functioning in our natural state which is doing things in the state of God's will. To add a degree of clarity to understanding the situation, you must know that God designed man in his own image and when functioning properly, this is pleasing in the site of the Lord. Years and years ago, Ezra, of priestly descent, complained about these issues in his chronicles, Paul lectured about the problems and suggested the utilization of the mosaic laws, Mark and Luke wrote books on the behavior of mankind. Somehow it seems that the desires for some temporary joys outweighs the joy that is eternal in nature. Understand that time is winding up and patience is wearing thin, yet we must acknowledge that it's never too late to surrender and began again. We as people of faith must continue to do God's will. The blessings of atonement are infinite. Degrees of darkness produces obstacles towards receiving God's grace and love. We must be thankful for His mercy, for within there is another chance. Within His will, Grace and Mercy will follow you all the days of your life. Grace be unto thee that love ye the Lord, for His mercy is everlasting, His grace is eternal, His peace is comforting, and His love is there regardless of our ways. As believers we must know that we are never alone because of His Omnipresence. As we live and breathe, give God the praise because He is worthy of this blessing! As we walk in His ways living the Christian life, we must understand that worldly ways are a thing of the pass. There should be no more worrying, pain, crying, loneliness, hatred, deceit, lying, killing, revenge, dysfunctional thought or judgment towards our brothers and sisters.

The Strength of Our Faith

When we encounter congregates that show up at the house of worship on Sunday morning in the sanctuary with gossip, attitudes, self-centeredness and judging others, jamming a little hard listening to the hymns, and placing drink orders to the ushers with the collection plates, catch them and bring them back to reality and let them know that they have entered the Lord's house of worship because there is that outside chance that they may think that they are still at the club from Saturday night. Is it possible that most of the chaos of the world is caused by immature Christians not showing the love of their faith? Remember that God is Love. Keep in mind that throughout your Christian journey, if you are expressing anything less than love, you could be causing some degree of chaos and confusion. In all actuality, know that it's your attitude that will give altitude to your blessings. Trust and believe in God's word because He represents love. What the world needs now is love more than anything. In a world that is full of chaos and confusion, whether the issues will make you stronger or weaker depends upon your level of faith. True atonement with the theism of such a powerful God can walk you through any type of trial because Jesus overcame the world. This will help you to mature and give you strength. Think about those Hebrew boys in that fiery furnace or even brother Daniel in the lion's den, faith kept them strong. Now when man steps away from his faith because of an angered spirit, he is in danger of hell's fire. Always acknowledge that as a person of faith, when we find ourselves in and angered state of mind, understand that the problem is not the person who provoked you to anger, it is actually you lacking maturity within the faith. True atonement yields such degrees of Joy that one can see beyond and angered State of mind. God is Love!

Be Ye Holy, for I Am Holy

There are Christian friends that are not celebrating Jesus as much as they should be. When one remembers where we have come from and realizes that things could have been another way, celebrations are in order. Now since you've converted with obedience, you should have noticed a change in your quality of life. Show some appreciation for His gifts through praise and worship. Offer praise with friends and share what Jesus has done for you lately! Don't ever take your eyes off the prize!!!

Let's Take Some Time to Actually Analyze the Status of America

A few years back we had a president that analyzed and determined that the current status was not working for the future of the American people. He realized that we could not afford the future that our heritage had paid into. The investments were made, the taxes were collected, the government was operational, but the records showed that we were overspending, efficiency was in question. Are there any of you out there that desire government vouchers rather than monthly checks for your social security benefits? Vouchers simply limited your liberties to spend as you please. The number of people about to retire was astronomically large and the retirement bill for Social Security was even larger. Fundraisers, budgeting and smart investments were all on the table in support of a successful transition beyond the Baby Boomer retirement event. We had to call on the name of Jesus.

There is strength in the name of Jesus. Know that those that have faith will no doubt receive power. Using this power to show love can prove unending. Mathews 21:21: "Jesus answered and said unto them, Verily I say unto you, If ye have faith, and doubt not, ye shall not only do this which is done in the fig tree, but also if ye shall say unto this mountain, Be thou removed, and be thou cast into the sea; it shall be done." These words can explain this more efficiently than the finite mind of one man. Personally, I think that we should consider the fact that God is our everything if we take a thorough look at His Omnipresence and His Omni knowledge and grace. Romans 1: 20: "For the invisible things of Him from the creation of the world are clearly seen, being understood by the things that are made, even His eternal power and God-head; so that they are without excuse." Step out on your faith today and know that God's blessings will come your way!

If it wasn't for philosophical and physiological thought, fire and brimstone could be the result. If we want to live amongst one another we simply would have to get along. The logic to the theology is that God's in His infinite wisdom, is in charge! I personally see respect, love, and mercy. Try to give God His praise and thanks today. Now you know that it could have been another way!!! GRACE! Those of you that are sadden, disenchanted, depressed or even ones that have lost their joy from some worldly issues, I must share this, 1 Peter 3:16: "Having a good conscience; that, whereas they speak evil of you, as of evildoers, they may be ashamed that falsely accused your good conversation in Christ." Know ye this day that it is only the demonic spirits imbedded in those that attempts to block mankind from the love of Christ. Trust these words. If you believe and acknowledge his will, God loves you and that is all that matters.

When one looks at humanity as one species and consider the fact that we are all either parents, siblings, cousins, nieces, nephews, aunts and uncles to one another, which is all family. It's hard to gain clarity and understanding of the chaos and confusion that is in the world. Since we are all family, we really need to show more love towards one another in the same way that God loves us. His forgiving grace yields peace every time. That's His plan. Keep in mind that God has a plan of action for our salvation. Our job is to follow His will and obey His words. At this degree of atonement there are many blessings alone with joy and peace. Now when life deals us problems that interrupts this joy and peace, we must consider the fact that we might be out of God's Will or disobeying His words.

With God's omnipotence, it is better to follow His will. Peace be unto thee that follow God's will. God loves you anyway through his forgiving grace for your sins. Existence yields peace when we love one another as God loves us. When you can acknowledge God's Omnipresence and how He has carried us from where it could have been for us, it makes us wonder where the strength is coming from that allows Christians not to do His will. Keep in mind that God is Love!!! It is in His will that we love one another as we love ourselves. Compliance yields peace on the horizon. Remember God is the only one able to judge because He knows all things. Give God the praise every chance you get simply because He didn't have to give us another chance.

God Overcame the World

For some, the hardest thing to live through is the death of a close relative. If you are a believer in Christ, then you are beyond the stain of death. Those that are standing as children of faith must keep in mind that God has prepared a place for us where we will see each other again. We must lead those that have not yet been converted with this knowledge and wisdom with a comfort to their sorrows from lack of understanding. Know that Jesus overcame the stain of death. Study God's words. When people surrender themselves to the spirit of Christ, the light of the world changes. The protection from the atonement of accordance will shield you from the heat of a sinful world. The heat from these sins cannot penetrate the atonement of God's love. All the worldly things that people hold on to after this conversion dims the light of atonement for them!!! To God be the glory and strength!

There Is Power in the Name of Jesus!

Have you ever needed support in a hurry and that relative that you have not seen in years had what you needed but was reluctant to help? This made you feel bad because it was family. As Christians, we must acknowledge that this happens more frequently than we realize! The situation usually works out a little different with relatives that you frequently visit. As Christians we must try to keep and open relationships with our Father in Heaven at all times so that when we call upon Him, He will answer expediently because of familiarities, and get you through these worldly times. Make friends with Jesus every chance that you get, He has the power and can see you through these trials and tribulations. Keep in mind that God is good. Study His words, He can see you through to peace. If man's arrogant attempts to destroy the planet, God in his infinite wisdom and power would possibly place creation back to the fifth day. Then He would possibly analyze what was not good and not very good. Those people that do not realize that the disenchantment of Our Father in Heaven has with the behavior of His children gone astray, trust and believe, our Father has the power to chastise! Try to do your best daily to help mankind enjoy the garden with its parameters and know that God is able. We must thank God for His forgiving grace because we have all fallen short of obedience to his words. Grace be unto thee that love ye one another and believe!

FYI, you must understand that it is because we love one another, it is that which makes us human. All else is just a sign of the beast with its death and destruction. Trust and believe that God is Love and it pleases Him that we do His will. Grace be unto thee that love the Lord. Be blessed this day.

In a world that is so full of chaos, confusion, death and destruction that was once perfect, how is it possible that man can be content with life? Jesus can make a way out of no way. He can turn your midnights into day. When you trust in Him, He will bless your stay.

Anytime mankind goes against God's plan and implement his plans, failure is imminent. Walk in His way and serve His will, the blessings will come.

In every situation that has been built with the foundation of a lie, the actual days of the existence are numbered. For the strength of the existence in any given situation, plan to build on the integrities of love and trust. Most anything else can be proven as darkness and will simply dissolve into the blowing wind. The divine nature of the Spirit of the Lord will not dwell around any degrees of darkness.

There is power enough in the name of Jesus to eliminate disenchanting spirits selling darkness. The significance of your accordance with God's words will determine how well you can receive strength from the light of the world in the name of Jesus.

Of all the things that one encounter during life's journeys, there is great significance in having a solid spiritual home foundation, especially if the world presents dark spirits that interrupt your atonement with your straight and narrow walk. Know that your familiarities with home will set you free! Jesus' words are the key.

Appreciation of a Great God

Let's us drop this into the hat of salutations; for many years, great men like our Pastors, Deacons, at least 40 biblical authors over a period of 1500 years have offered us guidance and leadership towards a peaceful existence full of Joy and Love all inspired by the Holy Spirit. Take a minute to examine 2 Timothy 3:16-17: 16 "All scripture is given by inspiration of God, and is profitable for doctrine, for reproof, for correction, for instruction in righteousness:" 17 "That the man of God may be perfect, thoroughly furnished unto all good works."

Bottom line is that when a child is given instructions by a parent and if they fail to follow these instructions, there is usually a punishment that follows. We must utilize good judgment. It was imperative that when man surrendered at conversion, we needed to release the trickery of the past to be granted the blessings of our future. To God be the glory!!! It is truly not wise to invest your time and desires into worldly things because these things become old when the new changes come. Now on the other hand, when you invest time in God's word which will never change, this is a wise investment because of its pure and divine nature. We must examine in life what is it that brings joy to the people of your environment. Be of good cheer, God's word is the answers to joy and peace. Every time I think about the goodness of the lord, I just want to give Him praise. He has never let me down. Even in my ignorance when the fellows said that brothers not right, He was my friend when He took the time to show me the way! During the times when I was down, thinking about His goodness built me up. In spite of the devilish nature of a trapped humanity, He showed me how to love, during my trials and tribulations where mountains of troubles stood, He showed me how to pray, and when my soul was threatened when I took my eyes off of the prize, my weaknesses in life, He showed me His power! God owns the plan of salvation! Give Him the praise!

The Worldly Rich Man Desires to Get into Heaven

Do you know how hard it is for a rich man to get into heaven? The mind of a rich man is always centered on worldly things which will deteriorate in time with change. Maintaining and atonement with the true light for blessings requires humility. The word says that the poor will be with you always and are always humble. If your ship comes in and you want to sit at the big table, first determine their logic. At the table of the Rich and Famous most of the time you will find chaos and confusion. Support those that believe and trust in God's words. Know that God's word will never change. Stability for humanity is at hand. Life makes it hard for a person when he is blessed with prosperity in a capitalist society while studying a degree of faith which demands humility. Actually, until you have matured within our faith and are atoned with God Our Father's master plan, you may encounter experiencing levels of selfishness, confusion from insecurities and facing the dilemmas of missing blessings! We must acknowledge the fact that mankind in his finite wisdom often makes decisions impatiently to meet a resolve through a sense of pride in His accomplishments. Our Father in Heaven is the light of the world, with His power and infinite wisdom, loves His children. Humanities disenchantment with global warming, poverty, wars, unjust incarceration, pollution, conspiracies and all other chaos and confusion while in darkness need to experience the light. This light is the answer to escaping darkness. Throughout and eternity life is exceptionally a short period of time. It might be wise to consider becoming a child of the King. There is power in the name of Jesus. Gather atonement by studying the word of God. There is always room in the Kingdom of

God. You do know that the minute that we put our religion on a shelf to indulge in some worldly activities or selfish endeavors for personal gain, God actually takes the blessings that we are about to receive and place them on another shelf.

Until we learn to let go and let God, we might frequently visit darkness and despair which is far from the purity of His marvelous light. Trust in Jesus for your desires and needs, He will lead you away from all degrees of darkness, His words are true and pure!

Taking Out the Trash of Darkness

The only way to free a mind is to know how to take out the trash. Know we must have a clear understanding of what the darkness of trash is. If one declares some degree of power that is less than one's physical strength, it's trash, take it out. If while searching for a solution to a problem, one is motivated with a determination to do evil, it's trash, take it out. If one monitors an associate and notices degrees of prosperity and happiness and one's mind is taken to enviousness, jealousy or deceit, it's all trash, take it out. If at some point in one's life the mind expresses desires to control other's thoughts to get them to do what you want them to do, it's trash, take it out. If at some point in one's life, there are thoughts that causes you to think that you are God, it's trash, take it out. All ways of darkness! You must understand that when your mind is free and clear, you can really hear what God is trying to tell you. The Garden is at hand!

Always know that God's word is true and pure, know that your opinion from the heart can change a life. Study to show yourselves approved. Share the purity of His Divine grace, which can supply our needs. We must acknowledge that when we are entrapped into committing evil acts, there are abnormal conditions occurring within our lives. Man is naturally good!!!

Our brains require oxygen to function properly. God created an atmosphere with oxygen in the first six days which was good and very good for mankind. Deprivation or lack of oxygen content can't be good.

The next time the world places you in a situation that causes you to lose control of your norm, stop, take a deep breath and turn it over to Jesus. He will make everything alright.

The Significance of Mankind

The significance of your existence is determined
by the number of people that you have helped during your lifetime.

The significance of the number of blessings that you receive is determined
by how well you learn to do God's will.

The significance of how well you can see the light of the world is determined
by how much of the world's darkness that you surrendered at conversion

The significance of how much of God's love you feel is determined
by how much you love God

The significance of how much you love and appreciate Jesus is determined
by how much you read your Bible and understand
how much He went through for you because he loves you.

Beyond the Darkness of the World

When I was a little boy, my family taught me how to count to ten. I thought that I was smart because a lot of my friends at that age could not count to ten. I am truly grateful because 98% of our existence has something to do with numbers and the other 2% is simply and impulse stimulus reactions.

When I became a young man, my Church family taught me the Ten Commandments which was written with a brilliance that effects all aspects of life. The peace that I have encountered with this knowledge has been such a blessing and has allowed me to rest. Within your lifetime, be of good cheer, study your Bible, knowledge is a blessing, know that Jesus holds the key to happiness and that he can make a way out of no way. God's words are still shining beyond the darkness of the world. The illumination from His Omnipresence demands your Humility! His everlasting love and grace deserve your praise. His blessings are beyond your imagination. You must know that you are fortunate to have such a great God. We as a people have the tendencies of wanting to walk after the flush. Within this state we experience the dilemmas of the flush. The theological spirituality of our faith offers a relief from these encounters. Glory be to God that He died and rose in the spirit of the Lord with all the power of Heaven and Earth in His hands. We should all consider walking in the spirit to allow this power to help us bypass these worldly dilemmas. At that point in our lives when we figure that the things that we have and enjoy so much because we think that we have achieved them on our own, we must first think, could it have been another way. Let's continue to give God praise and honor so that we can receive another blessing. You know He didn't have to do it.

Worldly Nature

How often is it that we allow the world to interrupt our relationship with God? At this point we walk away from the straight and narrow ways and away from God's grace. The Holy Spirit is always ready to bless us walking in the light of God's plan. We should never allow the darkness of the world to change us to where we miss our blessings. God's grace is enough to supply our needs. It is very important in a relationship to have a level of trust. We must know that trust offers the motivational stamina to build. Relationships lacking this stamina often see levels of deceit, distrust, destitute, prevarications, ambiguities and condemnation, all leading to an expiration date. We should always put forth our greatest effort to make our words be a bond to our actions, just as Christ has done for us after we were converted. His words have been a blessing. As we walk through this missionary journey, getting closer to Christ, we should come to the realization of how great God is. In all actuality, death, darkness and helplessness becomes a thing of the past, because of the atonement and power from the light. The true and Divine nature of His words will see you through. All from the living spirit of Christ.

Enjoy your blessings. Take time out of your busy schedule to give God some praise for being the ideal Father. He took the time to make a way for His children. He teaches us that the family is first, and He forgives us for our mistakes. What a great leader and friend to follow. I do know that without Him I would be less than the man that I am today. I challenge fathers everywhere to be this for their kids and watch them achieve greatness. When they arrive, place your life on hold, and help them to build their lives. This is how you set yourself up for a blessing. We must understand that some of the greatest mysteries of this faith are hidden from mankind to protect him. Usually mankind's destructive nature derives from less than a freed state of mind. The closer we get to this faith's logical functionality, the freer our minds get and the more power we receive. Daily, trust in the Lord and know that He is ready to bless you.

Following God's Will

With proper guidance, there can be peace on earth. It was no accident that the Sermon on the Mount was placed near the beginning of the New Testament, this position indicates its importance. In this sermon the King summarizes the character and conduct of His subjects. This sermon is not a presentation of the plan of salvation; nor is its teaching intended for the unsaved people. It was for the Disciples and was intended to be there constitution or their system of laws and principles that they were to walk with. The Beatitudes were meant for all past, present and future Christians who acknowledges Christ as King in their hearts as He reigns in Heaven. Always trust in the Lord for his leadership and guidance. In life, always try to be and encouragement towards enhancing the betterment of mankind. This is a part of God's plan. Know that God loves you, know that there is love in your heart, above all, know that God is love. You have to understand that if you have shared any time within this faith, you must know that there is no rest for the weary. If you didn't get anything else at conversion, get this, God's got your situation at the altar! In life one of the toughest lessons to learn within this faith is to forgive those that intentionally misuse you. Many say that the trouble you cause will be your trouble soon. Others say that without forgiveness the enemy controls you. At this point the darkness shows you revenge, deceit, and evil. We must understand that God's forgiving grace was what saved us, cause none of us really got what we deserved. In our quest to be more Christlike, our efforts bring praises unto Him.

Keep your mind stayed on Jesus. In the spirit of faith, always know that God is love. It is important to keep this in mind while evaluating the scriptures.

Regardless of the situation, enviousness jealousy deceit, revenge or greed, there is no scripture that provoke you to violence. Always walk in His way and grace will be unto you. One of the benefits of walking in the way of the Lord is that every now and then you get to fill the power of His might. The significance of those days when the darkness of a sinful world tries to engulf you, yet you walk away with joy and peace. When the tolerance of your patience is far beyond the understanding of worldly subjects. When you understand that He might not come when you want Him, but He's always there on time. To get peace in the valley we need Jesus. The secret to a productive consciousness is to never allow the world to enslave you. From birth, anything is possible if you set your path and stay on it.

The level of support you receive will depend upon how much support you offer society as a peaceful servant. The only way that you will enjoy your journey is that if you have love in your heart. All else is just a battle.

When You Have a Story to Tell

If you have a story to tell that will offer encouragement to the youth of today, please come out of your shell and let the truth be told.

So many of our youth are lacking moral and ethical fortitude and without the dynamics of humility, they are lacking the survival skills needed for a successful future. It's like someone dropped the ball with some of these kids.

I challenge you all to become mentors to the youth of today so that we can build a better future.

Let's all be aware that God didn't make anything evil. Understand that at that point when you find yourself doing evil, you probably have a shadow pulling you away from the straight ways of the Lord.

At this point you are blinded by this darkness and all motivational actions are illogical. Gather atonement with your faith in the Lord and follow His leadership. He has a plan for your life, and it does not include dark days. God is good!

One of the greatest pleasures in life is peace of mind. Let us put forth our greatest efforts to live by God's will and His ways because there is peace in the name of Jesus.

Integrity of Faith

The integrity of man's faith is determined by how closely he walks in the light of it. The weight of the world is detrimental to spiritual atonement because of the darkness. God's words tell us that we simply cannot serve two masters. Now for the possibility of blessings far beyond your imagination, choose ye this day whom ye shall serve. We must acknowledge that the spirituality of mankind is one of its greatest assets in a capitalistic society. Love, peace, humility, forgiveness, mercy, compassion, giving and sharing grace, these are all a part of this agape timeless spirit. Most worldly assets are lost with the passage of time and yet are adored in capitalist and socialist societies. Logic dictates that many assets are not worth it if they cannot withstand the passage of time. To clarify, as a child of God, walk in the spirit to experience the true values of life.

The Angered Spirit

Can we take a minute to attempt to meet a resolve towards anger? Let's first look at that point of conversion from a sinner to a believer in Jesus Christ. As a converted Christian follower, it should be our desire to do God's will that we might be blessed. As we study His words in our Bibles, we are taught that Jesus died and rose with the power of Heaven and Earth in his hands. His words also teach us that we should leave our problems at the Altar of Christ and continue to do His will. God's omnipresence yields the truth. Now can we through deductive logical reasoning conclude that the angered spirit is simply lack of faith?

Please keep in mind that we live in the world, we must understand whatever we experience God's got us. Grace be unto thee that love and walk in the will of the Lord.

God is love!

Prayer Works

We must keep in mind that prayer works. We must know that all exposure that draws you away from God's straight and narrow ways is darkness. Your faithful atonement should bring you back to where God wants you to be. Atonement to God's Will yields blessing. Note, everything belongs to Him. Please keep in mind that God loves you. Always do your best. Know that God has the power to change things if you call on Him. Grace be unto thee that calls on the name of Jesus! How magnificent is it to have words to study that enhances every aspect to the betterment of your very being? As our Father in Heaven loves you, He wants to bless you, the truth is expressed in His words. In a world filled with darkness, sin, evil and mistrust. God's got you, all you need to do is trust and believe! Peace be unto thee that love ye the Lord. Let's all consider the fact that the world must be corrupt because we all fail to love one another. Now our Father in Heaven has a master plan prepared for us and to receive the blessings from this plan, all we have to do is follow His will. Part of His will is that we love one another. There are blessings of peace and joy in following God's plan. Let's encourage one another and change the world to a better place by following God's plan. Throughout history, there has always been degrees of confrontation between the sinners and the matured faithful Christians. There are always the questions on whether Christians are spending more time judging one another, teaching the faith, condemning the sinner, or having a compassionate realization that God is still working on some of us. Always know that thee that has the Holier-than-thou attitude and lives on earth has a lie in his closet. Mankind has sinned and fallen short according to God's words. Know Ye this, that the salvation comes when your faith keeps the world from changing the amount of love in your heart. Love Ye one another!

His Name Shall Be Called Wonderful

We must be thankful for Jesus because without His will and His way, life would be full of chaos and confusion. How wonderful is that? We must acknowledge the fact that God is able because the theology was developed pure, without blemish, and this faith is accommodating for and eternity. The inconspicuously designed worldly nature that man is exposed to has no significance to who we are supposed to be. When we are weak and allow the nature of darkness to exist, changes to man's destiny occurs. Stay steadfast and immovable within your faith because there is strength in the name of Jesus. God has a blessing waiting for you. If you live long enough, it gets easier to grasp on to the fact that things could have gone another way! Let us all at this point in time give our Father in Heaven some praise for His Love and for keeping us. You must understand that there is peace after gaining Heavenly wisdom through God's words! Now most of our problems come when we try to serve two masters. When at conversion we approach the throne of grace with a glass half full of the world, the glass cannot be filled. When we refuse to surrender ourselves wholeheartedly to God's will we limit your blessings. Now Our Father in Heaven with His Pure and Divine nature with all degrees of the power in his hands is more than a conquer over this half empty glass. Let go and let God! When a man evaluates how it is that he expands the energy of his existence and decides that he wants to help someone every chance that he can, know that he is a naturalist and blessed. Be this and God will smile upon you! Be blessed today.

Conclusion

Please keep in mind that our God is our Salvation. Trust in the Lord. You wouldn't believe how many people out there that do not know that God can fix things regardless of the situation. He has the power of Heaven and earth in his hands. Grace be unto thee that trust in the Lord. If we walk in His way, the blessings will come.

In life, you would not want to be limited to being a worm when you can mature into a butterfly, being free to grow. Mankind must mature within the faith to be free.

We should never make attempts to judge because we don't know the consequences of our actions, all circumstances require knowledge and facts of the situation before judgement can be made. Life is so much easier if we just let go and let God. He has the power, knowledge and presence over all situations. We as faithful believers should give thanks to our Father in Heaven for His plan of salvation, because without it there would be no peace on earth, love in our hearts or good will toward men. We should give Him praise daily for His goodness. At that point of conversion from sinner to Christian faith, the more you give up, the more you receive. Faithful atonement yields blessings.

When mankind can live his life filled with peace which represents harmony. True harmony strengthens salvation. True harmony yields love. God is love. Within this harmonious society you should find evidence of mercy with scores of forgiveness. Even true friendship can be found because of the levels of meekness. We would be able to walk with understanding because of the type of caring, sharing and trusting of one another. By now you must realize that we are so far from this place that we should all study God's plan for our lives and pray daily without ceasing.

We must keep in mind that it was God's keeping power that brought us through. Let's all be thankful and give Him praise because things could have gone another way.

Consider offering Him praise for what he is about to do in your life. Know that God is able.

It really appears that the beginning of the end is on the corner, fire and brimstone down the street, death and destruction up the street, chaos and confusion in the homes, deceit, entrapment, lies, disrespect, dishonor, adultery, idol worshipping, killing and stealing all on the next block. But God, in his Omni presents, potency and knowledge with His forgiving grace has the whole world in His hands. In other words, for the love of His children, God's got this. Trust and Believe!!!

I would like to take this opportunity to encourage you all to give God His Honor and praise today and every day. I have learned that the atonement with the will and ways of our Lord yields blessings and strength.

At one point in my life there was such a corrupt spirit over me that kept my days full of chaos and confusion. Now since I have found a friend in Jesus, the joy and peace are blessings within themselves. These gifts are astounding with emphasis on the atonement to God's will.

I can say that I have experience firsthand coming out of darkness and walking into the Light! God is still working with me and I want to thank Him for not giving up on me.

References

1. King James Version, Holy Bible
2. The Church, Turnel Nelson

Education: Undergraduate work

1. The University of Tennessee - Knoxville, Tennessee
2. Rose State College - Del City, Oklahoma
3. Shelton State College, AE - Tuscaloosa, Alabama
4. Stillman College, BS - Tuscaloosa, Alabama

Ordained Deacon
Church School General Superintendent